"When I get scared, I just close my eyes very tight, very tight... very, *very* tight...and dream of sparkling stars."

Chloe, at age 4¹⁄₂

1

"This is a feel-good book. It kept giving me warm, fuzzy feelings while I read! We knew so much about being spontaneous when we were kids, but we forgot it all as we grew up. "Dance Naked" encourages us to reclaim those playful parts of ourselves while helping us find new options to deal with stress."

> – Kristy Marcus,
> Eating Disorders &
> Teen Issues Specialist

"This book is very sweet. With humor and softness, it gives us ways to deal in moments of stress. I was very touched by the open and non-judgmental way "Dance Naked" keeps reminding us to go back inside to connect and reconnect with ourselves and the earth."

> – Deborah I. Stark,
> Wilderness Guide

"This is just the kind of material we look for to use with people who have heart problems!"
— Maureen Devereaux, Cardiac Rehabilitation Therapist

"You can't help but pick this up! It is so fresh and energetic! At any page you stop, there's a great idea."
— Kathryn Peterson, Artist

"This is a book for anybody who's ever needed a break from a stressful day."
— Jonathan D. Natelson, J.D., Attorney & Financial Advisor

""Dance Naked' has a plethora of ways to remind real guys to stay connected with their feelings."
— Dennis Bohling, Furniture Maker

"A person with stress deserves this nurturing little book."
— William C. Gustafson, Doctor of Chiropractic

"This book gives us permission to get in touch with our innocence. How refreshing!"
— LeAnn Todd, New Project Development Manager

Dedication

I dedicate this book to the recovery of joy and to the teachings of the earth.

To my sister, Beth, who has been ever faithful to my work and who gives it beautiful form with her artistry;

To my daughter, Chloe, with whom I have been dancing since before she was born;

To my parents who gave me my start and who have their own dance;

And to all who have struggled with life, its challenges, and the process of growing wiser.

Dance Naked In Your Living Room

Other books by Rebecca Ruggles Radcliffe:

Enlightened Eating: Understanding and Changing Your Relationship with Food

Body Prayers: Finding Body Peace—A Journey of Self-Acceptance

About to Burst: Handling Stress & Ending Violence—A Message for Youth

Dance Naked In Your Living Room

written & illustrated by
rebecca ruggles radcliffe

EASE™ Publications, P.O. Box 8032, Minneapolis, Minnesota, 55408-0032 USA
Design & cover art by Beth Ruggles

Address All Inquiries to Publisher:
EASE™ Publications
P.O. Box 8032
Minneapolis, Minnesota, 55408-0032 USA
612-825-7681/800-470-4769

Manufactured in the United States of America

Alternative Cataloguing-In-Publication Data

Radcliffe, Rebecca Ruggles
        Dance naked in your living room:
handling stress and finding joy. Minneapolis,
MN: EASE, copyright 1999.

        1. Stress management. 2. Addiction—
Self-treatment. 3. Addiction—Prevention.
4. Self-help psychology.
        I. Title. II. Title: Naked in your living
room. III. Title: Handling stress and finding
joy. IV. EASE.

        613.5 or 155.9042
        ISBN 0-9636607-0-5

Library of Congress Number 96-090896

dear friends:

This is a book for all of us who learned to handle stress by copying others...and who consequently picked up some "bad" habits. Frankly, the habits we depend on have gotten us through difficult situations. But our overuse of eating, spending, working, smoking, drinking, aggression, gambling, isolation/pulling away, and sex has gotten us in trouble. These choices hurt our health, sour relationships, ruin finances, erode self-esteem, and diminish hope. Ideally, handling stress means finding ways to let off steam, acknowledge feelings, and express uncomfortable reactions—without being destructive to ourselves, others, or the world around us. There are many, many ways to do this. Yet we typically learn just one. Then we end up in trouble

and wonder why. No single strategy can handle all of our feelings and needs. So it's time to get creative. Each of us needs to find about 25 stress-management strategies (I call them *StressBreakers*™) that we can use no matter what we are feeling: mad, scared, frustrated, overwhelmed, lonely, bored, and so on. There are lots of suggestions in *Dance Naked In Your Living Room*. You may think of others, too. Make a list, carry it around in your billfold, paste it on the refrigerator or bathroom mirror, and refer to it when you get upset. This way, you won't have to overuse any single problem behavior. As you begin to rely on other ways to handle stress, those difficult habits won't seem so unbeatable any longer. I look forward to hearing from you with more ideas and reactions. All the best on this journey of personal discovery!

Warmly, *Becky*

Contents

 **1:**

Living In A Stressful World

The Set Up

High Stress Lives

The stressful nature of our modern life takes a toll on each one of us, every day. From the roads we drive on to the challenges we face at work and home, we experience high stress in our daily lives. Even news reports are filled with violent and hopeless images.

To get away from it all, we try quick and easy escapes: cracking open a beer; eating ice cream, chocolate, or chips; smoking a cigarette; getting high; having sex; buying something; yelling at others; burying ourselves in work; shutting everyone out; or taking a spin at the gambling wheel. These are not real solutions, and we know it. Yet the

majority of us use one of these outlets as our primary way to handle stress.

Destructive Solutions

Using these approaches now or then would not be a problem. But most of these "techniques" have a very negative down-side if they are overused. They destroy health, relationships, finances, and self-respect. So why do we keep using them?

It's simple. We don't have any other options. We don't know what else to do. We were never taught how to creatively and constructively cope with the stress of living—not in our families, not in school, not in

church or synagogue, not in college, and certainly not on the job. We learned by copying others when we were young. The adults we watched usually covered over problems and conflict using these same strategies because that's what they learned, too.

TOP 10 Over-Used Coping Strategies

Eating

Drinking

Smoking

Shopping

Working

Yelling/Violence

Isolating/Pulling Away

Having Sex

Getting High

Gambling

A Temporary Fix

Most of us learned at least one of the *Top 10 Over-Used Coping* Strategies on the list. They work! They provide an escape from our problems—at least for awhile. But in the long run, our old stand-by techniques get us into trouble when they are over-used: some are unhealthy, some of them are downright addictive, some are actually life-threatening, some of them destroy relationships, and some get us into financial trouble.

All of them can lead to a deep unhappiness with life, a lack of faith in ourselves, and sense of hopelessness about our fate and our ability to change it.

We need new choices. We need ways to let off steam. We need ways to handle the multitude of feelings that start churning in stressful situations. We need options that really work—so that we don't take our stress out on ourselves, the driver in the next lane, our spouse or companion, our children, our co-workers, or phone operators and store clerks.

Our Bodies Take A Beating

We cannot just wish stress away. When we are stressed, our bodies change dramatically: they gear up to fight or flee the scene. Every cell is flooded with special hormones. Our senses sharpen, our minds race, and we wait on edge, ready to respond.

When this happens day in and day out, we get enormously tired. Our bodies age, we get sick, and our spirits feel the burden of such a strenuous lifestyle.

Craving Release

No wonder we crave release. We want a break from it all. Even a few moments of peace seems better than nothing.

A quick smoke, a cold beer, or a smooth, silky candy bar do the trick: they take our focus off the problem for a little while. And our bodies settle back down.

No wonder so many of us try and dump out our stress any way we can. We yell at the counter clerk, our secretaries, or our children even though we aren't proud of it.

We try escaping—into our work, TV, a book, or our thoughts. Sometimes, we just leave to get away from it all—somewhere where no one can reach us. We don't want any more complications or trouble.

In such a stressful world, it is also easy to appreciate why we'd want to buy ourselves something new, try a few minutes at the slot machine, or take a turn under the sheets with someone. We feel as if we deserve a reward after all we've been through.

This also may help explain why drug use—legal and illegal—has skyrocketed. When stress is too much to handle, getting high feels better than reality.

A Harsher World

Sadly, we often justify our self-destructive behavior and unhealthy choices. If we feel better after we've eaten, yelled, gotten high, buried ourselves in our work, etc., then we assume it must have been the right thing to do at that moment.

We rarely consider what it is doing to our lives over time or how much stress we add to the lives of those around us when we do these things. Those who love us may worry about the unhealthy way we cope with stress. They may feel unable to help, cut off from us, or even dumped on. This causes their stress level to shoot up, too.

If we dump on others, be they strangers or those we know or love, it is not because they truly deserve such treatment. No one does. They are unfortunate victims just because they happen to be in the way.

Without knowing it, we have started a chain reaction. Now those we dumped on have to find a way to recover from our actions. To get rid of their stress, those we have hurt may in turn dump it on yet another stranger or someone they care for. The cycle spins out endlessly, making this world a cold and hard place in which to live.

The Intent To Change

We all contribute to this unfriendliness in our own way without meaning to. We are simply trying to cope with the stress in our lives which

often comes to us unfairly, too. How do we change the pattern? How do we handle stress more constructively? How do we keep from hurting ourselves and others? How can we contribute positively to our world rather than adding to the problem? Is this possible?

Yes, it is. But we must learn how. At present, each of us handles conflict the best way we know how. There is no blame in this. Most of us—including those who raised and educated us—did not have any emotional education. It is time to change this. Because if we don't learn new approaches to dealing with stress, we will kill ourselves early, destroy important relationships, and leave behind a world that is increasingly prone to violence and cruelty.

We need new choices. We need a way to find creative and constructive release from the inevitable stresses in each of our lives. In addition, we need to experience moments of joy. Otherwise, we get more tired and hopeless with each passing day.

Recovering Joy

Dance Naked In Your Living Room is dedicated to handling stress and recovering a sense of joy. It suggests alternate ways to unwind from stress. Often these are simple things that we do not think of as stress management techniques. But chances are, most of us don't think of our beer, long work hours, icy silence, TV watching, creamy cheese cake, frequent romances, etc., as stress management techniques either.

They are. They are the strategies we use to calm down. To get a load off. To feel in control again. *Dance Naked In Your Living Room* is full of alternative, more constructive choices. Some of them work when we are enraged. Others work when we are feeling alone. Still others work when we are panicked or frightened. No one technique will work for all situations.

New Choices

No Single Solutions

We need many, many different approaches to match the different feelings we have in stressful situations:

Angry	Frustrated	Ashamed	Lost
Fatigued	Empty	Guilty	Rejected
Confused	Panicked	Humiliated	Disappointed
Enraged	Betrayed	Inadequate	Lonely
Worried	Alone	Anxious	Overwhelmed
Bored	Afraid	Abandoned	

How could any one coping technique deal with all these feelings?
It can't. It just simply can't.

Yet we think that reaching for a cigarette, pill, snack, or drink will make it all better each and every time. We think that if we dive into a new project, new relationship, new store, new casino, etc., that it will make our problems go away.

Avoiding Dependence

No wonder it keeps taking more food, more money, more glitz, more power, more chemicals, and more risk to soothe us. We avoid our feelings, ignore the problem, and hope it will all simply vanish. It never does. And worse, we end up addicted to some chemical, behavior, attitude, or way of thinking.

To avoid getting hooked on something or to loosen a habit's grip, we need healthy substitutes—and lots of them. Armed with a variety of

strategies to match the range of complicated feelings we have as humans, we are less likely to find ourselves dependent on any one of them.

(And by the way, wouldn't it have been great if we learned this as kids? So, for those of you who interact with children, start teaching them new ways to handle stress so that they do not have to struggle with as many destructive behaviors or addictions as we all did.)

A StressBreakers™ List

I suggest that each person creates a list of 25 strategies that fits his or her personality and moods. Yes, 25 StressBreakers™! Using the strategies in *Dance Naked In Your Living Room* is a great way to begin. Then keep working to make it longer.

These 25 personal StressBreakers™ are the alternatives that we can use when we are all steamed up—or deeply frightened—or so bored we think we are going to go crazy—or so lonely we'd rather die than feel this way. These alternative choices are most helpful as interventions at the moment of crisis to help us calm down, to soothe our souls.

Once we are calmer, then comes the very important—and sometimes difficult—work of figuring out what is bothering us. Once we've identified what the trouble is, then we must try to find a constructive way to deal with the problem.

New Beginnings

A New Approach

To make new choices when we are under stress takes practice. But every one of us can do it. Let's take an example. Say you are leaving for home enraged because your boss treated you unfairly today. Rather than slamming your secretary or the security guard, harassing other drivers, pulling away from your family, or finding a way to escape, use one of the *Dance Naked* strategies to let off steam as soon as possible. (It's best to do this before you get home.)

Scream in the car. Write a nasty letter to your boss and burn it. Go for a hard run immediately after work. Play loud music. Go for a walk in a park. Read something inspirational. Call a friend and talk over the situation. Go hit balls. Then go home. This way, your rage will not be as intense when you interact with others.

Taking The Edge Off

These techniques will not solve the problem that got you upset in the first place—they will just take the edge off your feelings so that you can consider the problem and what to do about it afterward in a calmer state. You will still be upset. And if you do not deal with the problem, the agitation will inevitably return.

Make a promise to yourself to figure out a solution to the problem. That means, you must take time later in the evening—or certainly, within the next couple of days to search for a solution.

In this situation, a solution could be updating your resumé and switching jobs, filing a complaint with Human Resources, discussing your reactions with your boss, getting some therapy to deal with your feelings, drawing a picture of your boss and throwing darts at it, or learning Transcendental Meditation to keep your cool under pressure.

Honest Introspection
No one else can say what the best long-range solution will be in any situation except us. It depends on our needs. So when we take the

time to deal directly with a problem, we must be honest with ourselves about what our needs are, our strengths, and where we need to keep learning.

Difficult situations challenge us to become wiser. To figure out new solutions. To grow. This is how life works. We are not going to find smooth sailing. Rather, we must learn to ride through stormy weather.

Personal Wisdom
There is a silver lining: each time we rise to meet a challenge, we experience a special kind of satisfaction and joy from growing in personal wisdom. In fact, this is why so many traditional societies have honored elders for their accumulated wisdom. By learning to handle stress this way, we are reclaiming our own growing wisdom and inner strength.

Moments of Joy

Quiet Relief

As you use the *Dance Naked* strategies, you will find that many of them advocate pausing to discover small moments. Tucked into these quiet, small experiences, we often come upon unexpected moments of peace and joy. Usually we think of joy coming with big, life-changing events such as weddings, new babies, winning contests, holidays, and big achievements. But most days are ordinary—filled with routines, responsibilities, and challenges—not joy, peace, and contentment.

The demands of our day-to-day lives can begin to wear heavy on us unless we find some relief. We look for that relief when we turn to our primary strategy for handling stress (eating, drinking, working, etc.) But this kind of relief is superficial. It does not nourish our souls. And so, in the end, our over-used approaches to stress do not give us any real or lasting help.

A Sense Of Purpose

The relief we are looking for is deeper than that. It nourishes us at the center of our being. It reminds us that there is a reason for living. That our lives have purpose. That we are connected to the world, the universe. That we belong.

This sense of deep connection and purpose is very fulfilling. Even a small glimpse or a moment of connection can carry us for a long time. Often, these glimpses of deep meaning and connection happen in quiet, small moments. When we are by ourselves. When we are out in nature. When we have turned our attention to our inner selves. It is as if we have glimpsed the hand of the Creator, the Great Spirit. We perceive that things are just as they should be. We notice the incredible beauty of a birdsong, the color of a mountain at sunset, the sound of a lake lapping softly against the shore.

The Comfort Of Connection

A moment of joy has a way of comforting us, of assuring us that things are as they should be. We sense that there is a Higher Intelligence at

work behind the scenes, and that if we allow ourselves to be moved through our lives, a larger plan will unfold.

Moments like this are as vital to our souls as air is to our bodies. Without them, we live as empty shells, hopeless and despairing. With them, we gain the will to endure, to keep growing day after day.

Time To Listen

These moments come more often if we take the time to listen to our quiet, inside selves and to the mightiness of the universe in which we reside. We can put ourselves in the path of connection and let ourselves be nourished by the greater wholeness within and without.

Many of the suggestions in *Dance Naked In Your Living Room* get us out into Nature, encourage us to be silent, and point the way to inner listening.

Just having the openness to experience connection will often serve as invitation. Then a small moment of wholeness, peacefulness, or joy may happen. It can occur anyplace, anytime. After a workout. While sitting at a stoplight. While listening to someone's conversation. We cannot make them happen, but we can be ready to quietly notice and enjoy them when they do.

The Journey

Discovering Our Dreams

Dance Naked In Your Living Room is, therefore, a handbook for discovering creative ways to let go of stress and for noticing the wonder of simple things, the mysterious and potent silence of life which has the power to make us feel whole again.

Dance Naked In Your Living Room may help a remarkable journey unfold. Handling stressful situations will take attention and dedication, because it is much easier just to reach for that same old drink or dessert, cigarette or charge card, appointment book or remote control.

It is much easier to run away, yell away, gamble away, or seduce away difficult feelings. But this uniquely individual journey will lead us to learn new things about ourselves and where we fit in the world.

Deeper Feelings

Without fail, we will run up against feelings which we've tried to cover up. Such sadness, anger, frustration, loneliness, boredom, confusion, dejection, rage, emptiness, fear, terror, remorse, regret, and hatred are not easy to feel—especially since we seem to think we should be happy all of the time.

Yet even a drive down city roads brings up an assortment of unpleasant feelings: impatience, sudden fear, smoldering anger, arrogant

superiority, etc. Our family and work relationships bring up a much wider range of emotional reactions. Life problems involving health, finances, relocation, divorce, job loss, etc. all bring up much more emotional turmoil. It simply isn't possible to feel happy all of the time.

These so-called negative feelings are part of everyday living. Everyone feels them, even if they pretend they don't. But since we have labeled them bad and tried to deny that we feel them at all, we are totally unprepared and unskilled at dealing with them when they appear. We feel helpless and out of control in the face of negative feelings. Rather than learn a new way, we reach for our substance or behavior to shut down, cover up, and push away those bad feelings as soon as possible. Instead, when we learn to intervene in a new way to release stress,

identify the problem, and make appropriate changes in our lives, we enhance our power to change and create lives more in keeping with our dreams.

Living To Grow

Dance Naked In Your Living Room, then, is really a book about growing and honoring ourselves. It is at moments of stress and conflict that we find ourselves tested. We see where we need to make changes in our lives because of the unhealthy patterns and situations we are in. We see where we need to grow to improve the way we handle things. We may even become seekers because life does not unfold as we hoped or expected it to; so we look for new explanations.

Stress will kill our bodies—and our souls—if we do not learn how to creatively and constructively respond. We only have to note how many stress-related health problems people suffer from in today's world: heart disease, diabetes, migraines, indigestion, auto-immune disorders, addictive disorders, obesity, back problems, depression, neuro-transmitter dysfunction, etc.

The Dance of Life

Without constructive ways to handle stress, we begin to get pulled under by our repeated and incessant attempts to shut down feelings. When we shut down these inner signals, we shut down our lives. We shut down our souls. We muffle the inner flame that keeps pushing us

forward, giving us the will to live. Instead, we need tools to help us rise to the challenge and possibilities of our lives.

This is the dance of life. We come to it naked. The process of living strips us naked once again. No matter how much money, fame, control, status, education, or position we accumulate, it matters not in the face of stress. We respond from who we are, not what we have. We can be rich or famous and still be just confused or just as abusive to ourselves and others.

Honoring Our Inner Selves

The Challenge Of Growth

Dealing with stress shows us our character. Our inner essence. How wise we are. What we have learned. Our accumulated learning is what we take with us when we pass from this life. Growing is the very purpose for which we are here. So let us rally at the growing edges of our lives: those situations of challenge and stress that make us stretch to find new ways of thinking, make different life choices, or handle the unexpected.

Through this alchemy, we become changed. Wiser. Experience by experience. Until we leave this precious planet. Until then, let's *Dance Naked* in celebration, in contemplation, and perhaps sometimes even in desperation—depending on what each day asks of us.

Part 2:

StressBreakers:™
Creative Strategies For
Handling Stress

Dance Naked In Your Living Room

To bring the creativity back in your life, to feel free of other people's judgements or expectations of you, or to simply let everything go, shut the blinds, turn off the lights, put on your favorite music, strip off your regular clothes, and dance. Close your eyes and let the rhythm carry you. Find the beat and move with it. Quiet, wild, smooth, frantic, zany, deliberate, strong, primitive, earthy, romantic...it doesn't matter. No one can see. This is your time. Move your body. Let out energy. Express inner rhythms. Let your arms and legs go where they may. Find new moves, new possibilities. Dance, dance, dance until you cry, laugh, rage, feel the center, come to quiet, or fall down exhausted.

Swing To The Sky

There is a simple strategy available in many street corner parks or even right in our backyards for times when our hearts are weighted down by worries. It takes us back to feeling childlike, to memories of wind blowing through our hair, of looking at the sky framed by the points of our toes, of our first taste of freedom soaring high above the ground. The simple swing. What a great discovery! Even if our rumps have a tight squeeze fitting on the platform and we are not certain this feels comfortable anymore, it's worth a try. Push back and let the swing go. Feel the wind smooth away stress that fills you. Pump harder, higher. Close your eyes, and let yourself be carried. When you've had enough, let the swing come gently to rest. You can come back anytime.

Soak Your Feet

Sometimes, we get tired all the way to our feet. A good foot massage or foot rub can do wonders to revive us. So can a good, long soak at the end of a day. Any bowl or tub will do, and it can go anywhere: in front of the news, in front of a favorite reading chair, on the front porch while taking in the evening air, or in the privacy of a bedroom. Filled with hot water, with or without scent or soothing additives, our tootsies get a real treat. That soothing warmth stimulates blood flow, washes away the day, and relaxes the feet that work so hard. When our feet are happy, we feel better. In fact, in Chinese medicine, the feet contain a map of the whole body. Perhaps by treating our feet with care, we are actually bettering our sense of well-being.

A Good Book

There is nothing like a good story to take us out of our troubles for a while. A good tale can also teach us, give us new perspectives, make us think, and inspire us to endure or act more honorably than we might otherwise. Whether this tale is a western, mystery, adventure, fantasy, romance, historic novel, classic, science fiction, mysticism, biography, autobiography, or ethnic traditional tale does not matter. As long as it engages us and takes us into its midst, it will work. If it makes us smile when we put it down or think about it later and has characters to whom we can relate, then it is even better. Storytelling has been used throughout human history to teach, inspire, and give perspective to the lessons we face as we go through life.

Keep A Journal

Getting our feelings out, figuring out what is bothering us, gaining perspective on our problems, stumbling onto new solutions. . .these are all reasons for keeping a journal. We don't have to be great writers. We don't even have to finish sentences. We don't have to be polite. We can write what we can't say out loud. How therapeutic! We can put down a few sentences or many pages. We can journal every-day or just when we feel stuck or overloaded. There are no rules. This is a simple, inexpensive outlet that anyone can do anywhere. We can carry a notebook onto a plane, in a suitcase, briefcase, or lunch bag. We can write during lunch, before bed, first thing in the morning, while we are waiting somewhere, or on a plane or bus.

Turn On The Tunes

Whether it's loud, slamming rock and roll or a beautifully crafted concerto, music can soothe the soul. So when you find yourself agitated, lonely, confused, bored, angry, sad—(this strategy works with any mood)—get out your favorite album, cassette, CD, or radio and put on some music. Music works as soothing background noise or room-filling sound. It can be something you deliberately listen to or something you mix in with everything else you do. Notice how music affects you. Have music around that quiets you, some that makes you happier and more light-hearted, some that helps you cry, and some that gets you pumped up. We have many moods, and music can help with them all .

A Friendly Match

A good buddy to play with is a wonderful help when we are feeling bothered by things. The possibilities are many, but we need to get out and do something. It could be a round of golf, a friendly game of croquet, four-square (yes! what we played as kids!), tetherball, a tennis match, shooting hoops, bowling a few lanes, or tossing horse-shoes. When we play with friends, we feel nurtured by their affection, their willingness to stand by us, and their loyalty. If we feel like talking during our break, these buddies may give us a few words of wisdom. If not, we will return home later to deal with our problems, feeling *much* better from a healthy dose of joyful play.

A Poetic Word

Poetry speaks to and for the soul. When we are especially sad, wistful, confused, or grieving about something, writing poetry is a very healing choice. Poetry doesn't have to be perfectly composed. It doesn't have to be logical or sensible. It can be as moody and melancholy as we feel, and no one will criticize us for it. No one even has to know that we are writing our feelings down. When we sit to write poetry, we have a way to get our inner feelings all out safely and without judgement. The lines do not have to rhyme, but they can. And the poem can be short or long. As we struggle to express our most private and tender thoughts in the form of a poem, we often come to a deeper understanding of ourselves.

Build A Treehouse

Everyone needs a retreat. A place of his or her own. Kids know it and find small places for a fort or playhouse. It's time to remember that feeling again. So pick a tree. Get some lumber and hammer in the crossbeams. Sink footings if you need them. And then lay the floor. Now you have it. Embellish it with sides, walls, and a roof if you choose. Plain or decorated, it's your quiet private place. If you have a family, you can even take turns going to this retreat. If it's yours alone, then make this a special place for you. Add a candle, windchimes, sleeping bag, a few inspirational books, tape player, and binoculars... whatever makes this a place you can go and unwind. In any weather, any season, any situation. This is your private haven.

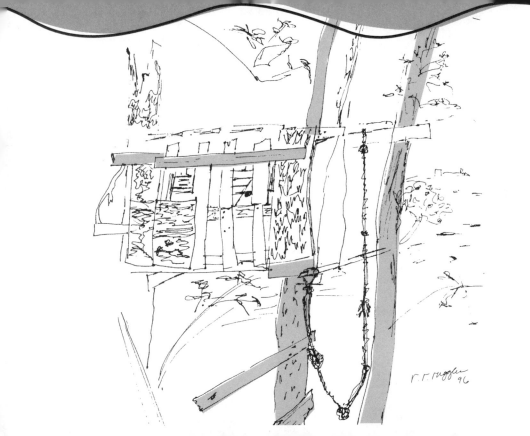

r. r. ruggles 96

Hang A Rope Swing

Find a strong tree, crossbeam, deck, overhang...anything from which you can safely drop a thick, chunky length of rope with a knot near the bottom. If you want, you can make a round or square plywood seat with a rope hole that rests just above the knot. Tie it on very, very securely. Make sure that the rope can swing in any direction freely without hitting anything or anyone. Then jump on and swing and twirl to your heart's content. Pretend your Tarzan. Pretend you are twelve years old again. Let go. Be silly. Most of all, breathe deeply and feel your body move.

A Cup Of Tea

Taking a few moments to make ourselves a cup of tea or cup of coffee is a wonderful way to unwind and take a short break. No wonder coffee shops are so popular. Historically, the Japanese knew the power of a tea ritual and elevated it to a spiritual practice. British "High Tea" brought refreshment to the end of an afternoon. In fact, many teas are thought to have specific soothing qualities. Having a cup of coffee or tea at the kitchen table, over our desks, in a bistro, on the front stoop, in our cars, or in a big easy chair, is a warm, soothing, quick, easy, and inexpensive way to take pause from the demands of our over-stressed lives. For those few moments, we let go of our cares.

Have Dinner With Friends

Gather a group of friends: people you know from the neighborhood, work, church, clubs, schools, etc.—and either go out to a restaurant or potluck at someone's home. These are people who care about you, who will listen to your concerns, will laugh with you, will be indignant for you, and who will give you a sense of connection. Put on great music, serve hors d'oeuvres, enjoy some cold beer or wine if you choose, and you've got the setting for a wonderful time. Regular gatherings such as these are important for feeling part of a community. Since our towns have gotten so big with families living around the country, we have to make our own communities. And what a great way to let our hair down!

The Love Of The Game

From gin rummy to Monopoly, games are a great release. Clearly, a game has to fit our personalities. Some people can spend hours playing gin rummy or bridge. Others find this too boring. Some love board games such as chess, checkers, or Risk. Others enjoy charades and other party game; still others would rather play something more contained or individual like solitaire or cribbage. Nonetheless, games intrigue, challenge, and entertain us. They sometimes get things moving, and help us connect with others. And always, playing a game lets us take a welcome break from the things that are burdening us.

Take An Outside Break

Tension and stress do not always hit us at convenient times. Often, we are at work or in conflict situations when we could really use some relief. Perhaps the easiest way to deal with stress in such situations is to get up and go outside for a lunch or coffee break. If you really need a get-away in the middle of the day, take your lunch or coffee and find a place to sit down for a mini picnic of sorts. You can sit in your car, on a bench at a park or bus stop, on the curb, or even on the grass. What a contrast from that tough environment! You're out in the air, feeling the breeze, with the sky open overhead, and the clouds passing by. You don't have to talk to anyone, explain anything to anyone, perform for anyone. You are free to just be. Drink it in and go back refreshed.

Learn To Juggle

When all the balls of your life are up in the air and seem about to crash, take out three balls (or stuffed animals, foam sponges, etc.) and learn to juggle! Try it! It may sound silly, but getting three balls into a synchronized circle takes some focus. This is just the thing to untangle tension that grips both minds and bodies. Start by simply tossing one ball in a gentle arc from hand to hand. Then add a second ball going in the opposite direction one right after the other. Just getting this down is a real accomplishment! If you dare, add a third ball to one hand and toss it just before you catch the ball coming from the other hand. (Get a guide book from the library or ask someone to teach you). You'll get a chuckle out of this and so will those watching!

The Sweetness Of Sunrise

At early morn, mystery still predominates. Quiet still hangs thick. Only the birds have stirred. As the sky lightens, we witness a mystery that has moved humans since the beginning of time. Over the horizon comes the giver of life. The source of power. That which shatters darkness. At first, there is only a hint of what is to come. A sense of innocence in the air. Anticipation. Birds bustle and chirp. Insects twitter. Light intensifies. The sky fills with pinks, yellows, and brilliant oranges. Our hearts eagerly wait for the edge of the sun. Then comes the great renewer! Day after day, we awaken to be nurtured on this planet. Sunrise helps us find a way to keep the mystery alive, our choices healthy, and our lives connected to the whole.

Watch A Sunset

There is nothing so extraordinary as watching the sun set at the end of a day. As the sun moves closer to the horizon, the sky goes through miraculous changes. How do painters capture such incredulous beauty on canvas? Slowly, moment by moment, the sun drops lower and lower until it vanishes over the world's edge. In this quiet closing, we have the chance for slowing down. For breathing more deeply. For sensing closure, loss, and mystery in our lives. Ultimately, we are here for such a short time. Yet a single day can sometimes be such a trial. At sunset, we may broaden our perspectives, seek for deeper answers, or simply surrender in the presence of a power that is clearly beyond our everyday lives. This one is free to all anywhere on the planet.

A Change Of Scene

Getting up and off our duffs and changing our usual routine can be very healing. It can jolt us out of ruts, change our mood, and give us a new way of looking at things. Too many times we get into a pattern and stick to it like glue because we are afraid to change. Try something different: take a class; try a new form of exercise; go to an afternoon movie; plan a weekend get-away; eat breakfast in the evening. For an immediate change of scene, simply get up and out of the situation you find yourself in. Leave the house. Walk around the block. Go for a drive. Go to a friend's. Run an errand. Taking a short break is especially useful if you are in an uncomfortable situation that you cannot leave.

Down & Dirty

Sand, mud, a leaf pile, or child's sandbox will do for this one. Get prepared to get your clothes and fingernails dirty. Set your rear end down into the earth for an instant return to childhood. Look around for essentials: broken sticks, pebbles, pieces of wood. Now start shaping designs, roadways, mighty castles, deep caverns to Earth's center... follow your impulses. Nothing has to mean anything. Nothing has to be perfect. Any structure can be demolished in an instant and begun anew. This is a good way to get grounded, to feel stable after something unsettling. If you're angry, you can create and destroy with great viciousness and it won't hurt anyone. And what a fantastic way to get in touch with our creative, more artistic (but often shy) sides!

Fix What Is Broke

Having something constructive to focus on while we try to sort out our own feelings can be very helpful. This may be the perfect time to do a project you set aside: sharpening kitchen knives or a lawn mower blade; repairing a bicycle tire; replacing burned-out light bulbs; sewing buttons back onto your clothes; bringing a broken chair or lamp to the local fix-it shop; gluing parts back onto kid's toys; getting a headlight replaced on the car, painting the bathroom. None of these things are earth-shattering tasks, but they give us time to think and settle down. We also get the satisfaction of taking something off of our "To Do" lists.

Lemonade For Sale

Responsibilities often close in on us and leave us heavy-hearted and with little joy. However, we are often presented with small opportunities to assist someone—and in return, find ourselves feeling a little better ourselves. Think about what it feels like to stop at a lemonade stand and make a child's day. It takes only five minutes and 25 cents to make a child beam with pride and gratitude. And we feel like a million dollars for being so nice. Or we can throw a ball back when it rolls into the street. We can open the door for someone elderly, injured, with a stroller, or with too many bags. We can give up our seats on the bus. We can pay someone a compliment. Small deeds of kindness are returned manyfold by how they make us feel.

Count To 100...or 1,000!

This classic method of letting off steam is told by many mothers or grandmothers to the youngsters around them: "When you are really mad, before you say anything, count slowly to 100." It seems silly and too simplistic. But when we are about to spout off at the mouth and say something we might regret, taking a breath and counting gives us pause. We have a few minutes to reconsider whether it is appropriate to let loose at someone or whether we have other choices. If we get to 100 and are still hopping mad, we can keep going! It helps to walk away for a moment to get our bodies moving and to prevent feeling trapped, too. When we come back and are done with our count, chances are, we will be a bit calmer as we face the situation.

Healing Gardens

Gardens can be one small pot or planter, decorative yard edgings, or whole plots of flowers or vegetables. Whatever the size, planting a few seeds or seedlings and caring for them brings us back to the simple beginnings of life. It reminds us how important attention is. How important simple nourishment is. With care, our gardens thrive. We feel the earth. We watch our small, tender sprouts push up and through with determination. They need us. If we forget to water them or give them light, they wither. So do we. Planting and caring for a garden teaches us how to care for ourselves. The same tender, quiet, and regular attention to basics helps us thrive, too.

r.r.ruggeri 96

Buy Yourself Flowers

It is amazing how much a splash of color on a kitchen table, dresser, desktop, or bathroom vanity can lift one's spirits. This simple indulgence doesn't have to cost more than a dollar or two. Go to a flower market that sells flowers by the stem. Wander and identify the colors, shapes, and smells that please you. Check the prices and choose one or more that you like and can afford. Some varieties last a very long time. Mums and daisies will add color to your environment for many days. Some flowers can be kept and dried so that your enjoyment continues. Each season brings new varieties and possibilities for adding a touch of beauty to your surroundings. Flowers remind us of the simple beauty of Nature to which we are all connected.

The Silver Screen

When feelings are churning inside and it seems impossible to make sense of them, taking in a movie at the theatre or at home might be the perfect strategy. A powerful movie has a way of bringing us into its midst where we identify with characters, and respond emotionally to its twists and turns. A good movie can make us laugh, cry, cheer, yell, gasp, cringe, and even think about it later. If you are in need of an emotional release, go to a video store or pick up the entertainment section of the paper and think about the movies you see offered. As you consider the choices, see if any particular one jumps out at you or catches your attention more strongly than others. Following that instinct may take you into an opportunity for emotional release.

Pound On Pillows

This is a fabulous, inexpensive, private, let-it-all-hang-out method for getting out anger or rage. These two emotions can be very destructive and frightening if we use them against others. Gather a stack of bedroom, couch, or sitting pillows. It's best to clear the room so that you don't shock anyone, and to feel as uninhibited as possible. You might even want to warn others not to be concerned about the noise. Now: punch, toss, kick, twist, and pound those pillows to get your anger out. Yelling and screaming into the pillows sometimes helps. For those of us who are not used to expressing anger, the intensity of it may be surprising. It is even possible to find ourselves crying as we uncover deeper levels of hurt or sadness.

Clean It Up

Since cleaning is such a powerful strategy for when we are grumpy or out-of-sorts, angry or devastated, confused or overwhelmed, we may want to leave a messy drawer, closet, or desktop for just such a time. Tearing through a tangled mess and bringing it to order can be immensely soothing when we are all churned up. Whether it's grungy bathrooms, a crowded storage room, a grimy kitchen, or a disheveled house, tackling the mess can be very therapeutic. When we get rid of dirt, put things in their place, throw out garbage, and make a space useable, attractive, and comfortable, it is very satisfying. It also gives us a chance to sort through thoughts and feelings on a quiet, inside level. This often happens almost without our realizing it.

Get A Massage

Stress accumulates inside our bodies, tightening our muscles, and winding us up tight as a drum. Over the years, this can lead to back problems, aches and pains, headaches, insomnia, and other stress-related ailments. One very accessible remedy is to get a massage. For roughly an hour, a professional works on muscle tissue and fluid balance to loosen up tight areas and get the blood and energy flowing again. For that whole period, we are the center of attention. There are no distractions. We leave behind our responsibilities. They will be there waiting after the session, but for now, this is our time. In a world in which we move so fast, such a slow and tactile experience can be very healing.

Take A Bath

When things seem overwhelming and too much to deal with, sinking down into a hot bath for a delicious soak may be just the thing to wash away tension. This is a private place. No one else can hear our thoughts. As the water relaxes us, we can go over the problems in our lives or simply let them go for just now. While this may seem like a small indulgence, the simple act of getting clean, slowing down, and allowing oxygen to circulate freely as our warmed-up capillaries open and improve blood flow, will change how we feel. A bath won't solve our problems, but it will help us deal with them better. Many find that adding bubbles, scents, candles, dimmed light, soft music, or a glass of wine increases the soothing quality of a private bath.

Pet Therapy

Taking a few moments to play with or care for a pet bird, cat, dog, hamster, chicken, mouse, guinea pig, snake, rat, horse, pig, goat, cow, sheep, or turtle can be very soothing. Pets love to be touched and talked to. Many pets return our attention and affection unconditionally. Their enthusiasm, devotion, affection, and lack of resistance is very healing for everyone. "Pet therapy" is very effective for depression, loneliness, and agitation. It doesn't have to be our own pet. We can go to a pet store, volunteer at an animal shelter, visit a petting zoo or farm, go to a friend's house where there are animals, or pet-sit for somebody.

A Soothing Scent

Humans have long known that scents have an affect. It is why we use perfume and after-shave. They please us, and we hope they please others. Now, aromatherapy is growing as an area of interest for more people. As our knowledge of herbs and plants increases, the range of scents on the market keeps expanding. At any bath, natural foods, or herbal medicine store you can find concentrated oils with a multitude of scents. It is fun to find one you really like. Put a drop on your wrist or neck to smell it through the day, or add some to a bath and come out with a very light aroma. Using it in a small burner will float the scent through your home. For fun, look up the qualities associated with that smell to see how it might be helping you.

Meditate To Transcend

Taking a meditation break once or twice a day for twenty minutes or so really helps center us and make us more resilient. In our fast-paced world, we rarely take time to slow down. Both our bodies and minds feel the effect. Slowing down, if only for a few minutes is highly beneficial. In fact, research has shown Transcendental Meditation to have very deep and beneficial effects which last even as we zoom back into activities. How surprising: we take time out of the day to be more effective during the rest of our activities. If our lives are very demanding, it may seem impossible to make this time. But if franticness never ends, it wears us down and ultimately makes us less effective. Renewing ourselves in quiet meditation is very powerful.

Buy Yourself A Gift

While some of us go overboard and get into trouble with shopping by going into debt, others of us never buy ourselves anything. It seems too impractical, indulgent, selfish, or self-centered. A purchase does not have to be extravagant. A two dollar gadget might be just the thing. A new book, new underwear, or houseplant could make us happy. As we wander through shops, our focus is taken away from the intensity of our situation. When we buy something, it demonstrates we are deserving. Buying ourselves a gift can be very comforting in brutally stressful situations. So if you find yourself feeling blue and needing nurturing, going shopping can be a wonderful way to treat yourself. However, remember to stay within your budget!

That Special Card

When we need to feel perked up or need a few words of inspiration, browsing through greeting cards is a simple solution. These days, greeting cards come in so many styles that if we need humor, we can find it. If we need words of wisdom, we'll find them, too. Taking a few minutes to read cards can pull us out of a slump and remind us that we are not the only person who finds this process of living a challenge! If we find a card or two that really hits home, we can buy them for ourselves. Carrying one in a handbag or briefcase or tacking one up by our desk or mirror can re-inspire us every time we glance at it. Besides, we may find cards to give others for upcoming birthdays, anniversaries, holidays, and so on.

Wild, Wacky Fingerpaint

If the problems we are struggling with are very weighty and grownup, they can overwhelm us. We may not be able to see our way clear. This is the time to be a little zany to break the tension—and to get our creativity going. New solutions come from new thinking. A few tubes of colored finger paint and some clean white slippery sheets of paper are all we need to get started. Prepare to get messy! The fun of this one is putting your whole hand in the paint. Use your fingers to swirl, whirl, criss-cross, and make tracks across the paper. Pat, push, plop, and simply be as silly as you want. Watch out. . .you may even find yourself giggling!

Call A Friend

When things aren't going our way, a kind and caring ear can make us feel less hopeless or stuck. Just giving voice to what is bothering us relieves tension. A friend's comments or perspectives may also help us consider our predicament from a fresh angle. One conversation can make such a difference. Some of us can reach out to others easily, and we have several people to call. Others of us have been taught to handle things in private and do not like to burden others. But keeping everything inside isn't healthy. Remember, if someone listens to us, we can return the favor by listening in turn. If there is no one around when we need to talk, many communities have hotlines. A drop-in center, pastor, or rabbi can also help.

TICKETS

r.r.ruggles '96

Patronizing The Arts

Humans have been trying to explain and understand their experiences since they began painting pictographs in caves. Art today still strives to do the same thing. Painting, poetry, theatre, music, film, and dance are various mediums in which artists tell stories, illustrate experiences, and evoke feelings to inspire and give insight. When we need some insight, it's time to visit an art gallery or museum, go to a poetry reading or play, or attend a film or concert. The music, lyrics, images, characters, and words take us into another world. We witness how others solve problems similar to ours and feel renewed. Besides special events and shows that come to town, art events are often hosted by libraries, schools, and non-profit organizations, too.

Affirming Our Dreams

Each of us dreams deeply about our lives. Reality often falls short of our dreams because life is so challenging. Yet, we continue on with hope—or resignation. If we resign, depression creeps in and we just bide time. This hateful and empty way to live merely fuels addictions. We are dreamers at heart. To feel alive, we must honor dreams, however impossible. Striving toward a dream acknowledges the creative intelligence we have inside. We need encouragement! Affirmations— simple, uplifting phrases that are particularly meaningful to us—can be posted to catch our eye, carried in a wallet, or repeated throughout the day. We can make our own or use a book. They guide us, help us believe in ourselves, and remind us we are not silly for dreaming.

A Friendly Visit

In the midst of our global village, many of us live as islands of loneliness. Gone, mostly, are small communities in which generations of the same family lived altogether. . .where people saw each other every day and knew how everyone was. Today, we live more isolated, dependent on a small family or circle of friends. When moves, divorce, illness, or death take their toll, we are often at a loss. When we feel alone, it's time to reconnect with those we care about. Calling a friend or family member and making a date for dinner, card game, or short visit is a powerful antidote to loneliness. If we don't know anyone, it is time to get acquainted. Join a club, have coffee with someone at work, volunteer at a nursing home, or mentor a needy child.

Historic Mentors

We are lucky to have the lives of many powerful men and women who have made a difference in the world captured in biographies and auto-biographies. Reading the life tale of someone who struggled under his or her circumstances, is often very helpful for keeping us afloat during our own struggles. Even reading a few minutes before bed or a few chapters on the weekend adds a perspective to our lives that we might not otherwise have. Most of us do not consider that we are right now in the process of creating a new chapter of human history which future generations will look back upon to learn. The issues we struggle with today—that often cause great stress—may be the very things that will change as we seek to improve our lives and the world around us.

Soothing Repetition

When noises or motions are repeated over and over, they can provide a very soothing influence. Watch a flower wave back and forth in the wind. Listen to water rippling over rocks. (Today, there are many small, inexpensive fountains available for rooms or yards.) Turn on a metronome to set a steady back-drop of sound. Watch a lava lamp change shapes endlessly. Listen to wind chimes. As we hear repetitive sound or watch repetitive motion, it permits our brain to shift to a different layer of functioning. We move more into an alpha-rhythm brain pattern, which gives us a creative, less linear way of thinking. We might feel like we are spacing out, when instead, our deepest, creative brains are cooking up new solutions and new perspectives.

Pick A Peck

During the growing season, get yourself off to a farm or orchard for a great day in the fresh air. This is a wonderful tonic for those who are overwhelmed with responsibilities. It is a great antidote for depression. It brings us close to Mother Nature, reminding us how the Earth gives us life and the responsibility we have to care for it. It brings us back to simpler times. Just putting on our grungy clothes lets us gear down. It usually means a drive into the country where the air is fresher, the earth is less crowded, and the basics take precedence. Whether we are picking raspberries or strawberries or harvesting bushels of apples, we get to sample fresh-picked produce on the spot and take more home. This is a slow, deadline-free activity that is sure to please.

Down A Hill

Remember the complete delight of taking your body twirling down a hill? The sky and ground whiz by as you turn faster and faster the further down you go. Any day you need to feel free from heavy responsibilities, or need to laugh and scream, this is a great outlet. Find a hill in a park, backyard, schoolyard, or deserted roadside. Get to the very top and take it all in. Notice the softness of the air, the unlimited sky, the grass below your feet. Now, get onto the ground and lay sideways, arms above your head, ready to push off. Then, simply roll a turn or two toward the bottom and before you know it, you are bumping crazily along like a log down a river, gaining more speed as you go. Do it again, and never mind the grass stains!

Royal Pampering

When responsibilities are piled sky high, it may be time to check in for an hour or two—or even a weekend—at a local spa. These days, spas are available in many metropolitan areas, not just at fancy national retreats. Look for anyplace that offers indulgent and relaxing mud baths, facials, jacuzzis, massages, delicious food, and a peaceful atmosphere. Whether you choose to have an oil rub, a complete make-over, or a stimulating shiatsu massage is really up to you. You may be invited to join in on a yoga or tai chi class, walk among flowers, or listen to peaceful music. This is a getaway in which you and your body are the center of attention and the purpose is to make you feel relaxed and pampered.

A Lump Of Clay

When there is no way to tell someone what you are really feeling without losing your job, breaking up a relationship, or damaging someone's self-esteem, you can push and shove at a lump of clay. This can be your hidden weapon against stress which you keep in your desk or kitchen drawer. No one need know. But when you have to pound, get the clay out to pull and tear, poke and chop, twist and crush all you want. Just a few minutes of "clay therapy" can give you an important outlet before you blow your top or do something which you later regret. Or use it in front of the TV, and you can work out all the knots in your day.

A Hard Workout

When frustration, anger, and rage start churning out of control, get yourself to a health club, running trail, or bike path as soon as possible. After warming up, hop on that stair-stepper, bike, rollerblades, running path, or ski machine and give it all you've got. While you have to be respectful of your body's capabilities, this is the time to work at the top end of your usual routine. With every step, stride, lap, or stroke, tussle with those feelings. Meanwhile, you can talk inside your head or under your breath about what's triggering your anger. This is not the time to stuff feelings or anything else. Express them through movement—privately, without hurting anyone, until you can see another way of looking at things or find a solution.

Go For A Walk

Walking is such a wonderful strategy because it can be done almost anywhere by anyone. Although we have to keep issues of safety in mind, going out for a walk to sort through what we are feeling is immensely helpful to many people. Walking gets our bodies moving. This helps feelings get unstuck. Walking also gives us something to do with nervous energy or agitation. It can lift up depressed spirits. It gets us out into healthier environments, full of fresh air and sunshine. We are made to move, to be outdoors. Yet most of our lifestyles keep us indoors and sedentary. So whether our walk is leisurely and meditative or fast-paced and deliberate, walking gives us time to go over what is bothering us and think through what we might do about it.

Stretch Out The Kinks

Our modern lifestyle gets us stiff and out of sorts, both mentally and physically. As we churn with inner stress, our bodies take a beating. Our neck tightens, our back and legs cramp, and our head aches. These are not signs of healthy bodies: they are symptoms of a stressful lifestyle. A morning or evening stretch is a very potent remedy for this kind of on-going stress. It is also a great release if we are over-whelmed with any emotion from sadness or confusion to frustration, etc. You can use any familiar athletic stretches or learn the beautifully simple bending sequences of beginning hatha yoga. The secret is threefold: Go slowly. Hold the stretch. Do not cause yourself pain. Isn't this a wonderful metaphor for life?

Desk Athletics

Long hours at a desk is a formula for fatigue and body tension. Add deadlines, office politics, and tough decisions, and it's stress overload. When we don't have time to walk, run errands, call a friend, or read at a break, we need short, quick remedies to do at our desk. Try these: roll your head in circles first one way, then the other. Stretch your chin onto your chest and then back as far as comfortable. Roll your shoulders forward and back. Circle your ankles both directions. Sitting down, run on your tiptoes as fast as you can. Squeeze your rear-end muscles tight and then release. Stand up and stretch from side to side. Reach your arms up over your head and then down to the ground. Now shake out your hands and legs, take a breath, and get back to work!

Shoulder Dancing

Shoulder dancing in a car is safe, legal, and a fabulous release if you are caught in traffic or you need to unwind in a hurry before you get somewhere. All you need is a radio and two hands firmly on the wheel. Turn your dial until you find music you like with a great beat. Oldies are often good choice. So is country and rock and roll. When you find a tune you especially like, start dancing. You'll be amazed at how many ways you can move your upper body in time to the music. Get that head going. Tap your fingers. Move your shoulders and even wiggle from the waist. Never take your eyes off of traffic, and keep a grip! But let a playful, creative, and downright gritty side of you come out. Hardly anyone will see you, and no one knows who you are anyway!

The Power Of Breathing

All of us know how to breathe, and don't think much about it. But as we get tense, our chests tighten and our breathing gets faster and shallower. Some people even hyperventilate. We get less oxygen for clear heads, and that means less energy to cope. So, whether we are at a desk, in the car, at home, in a meeting, or even in the middle of an argument, we can quietly notice our breath. First, take a deeper breath or two from the belly, not the upper chest. Notice the air flowing in and out. Let the lungs completely empty, and then take in a complete, full breath. Close your eyes if possible and simply follow your breath in and out until you feel a greater sense of peacefulness.

Swim Like A Fish

Swimming in water is one of the most soothing ways to release stress. We slip our bodies into the water of a lake, ocean, river, or pool, and let go. The water holds us buoyantly, with a fluid motion. As we gently glide through the water, we are enveloped in something restful, playful, primitive, and so familiar. After all, we are made of water. We take shape in a watery substance inside our mothers. Going for a swim immerses us in this life-giving essence and reconnects us to our origins. We move effortlessly, free of gravity. With eyes closed, the world goes away. All we are left with is the motion of the water and our inner feelings. Slowly, with each stroke, we can think through the issues we are facing and find a way to deal with them.

A Moment Of Prayer

A few minutes of prayer can sow seeds of much-needed faith to persevere through the situation at hand. While people across the world pray differently, all use prayer as a way of communicating with Divine Intelligence however they conceive of it. Communicating with a being, force, energy, intelligence that is larger than all that is human is comforting. It makes us feel like we belong. Like we have purpose. Like there may be a reason for what we are going through. We can pray with eyes open or closed. We can pray in the car, office, home, sidewalk, hallway, or park. We can use traditional prayer or make up something. No matter whether prayer is quiet and meditative, angry and confused, or boisterous and celebratory, prayer can help us.

Start A Collection

If you find yourself intrigued with anything from sports cards or antique muskets to teapots or woven baskets to coins or crystal, having a collection of things that interest you deeply can be very stimulating. When we are upset, taking time to sort or display a collection or searching for new additions can help us unwind. We need creative and constructive distractions. Working with a collection is a perfect outlet. A collection begins with one piece that we really like. If we stumble onto a second piece, then the collection is well underway. There are no rules for how big or how fancy. A collection is something to please us. If it is lace doilies or wildlife paintings and no one else seems to like them, so what? We do, and that's what counts.

Curing Cabin Fever

Sometimes we feel trapped by cold or bad weather and feel edgy from being holed up inside. Add this onto daily stress, and it makes cold months extra tough for many. They need not be. Get outside! We have become weather wimps with climate-controlled homes, offices, buildings, and cars. But our bodies are built to adjust. So add a few layers, and take the plunge! Walk in the rain. If you are lucky enough to live where there is snow, remember the fun it can be. Go sliding on a piece of cardboard. Build a snowman. Make snowballs and smash them against a wall without windows. Go skating. Learn to cross-country ski. Build a snow fort. Or just go for a walk. Listen to the birds, feel the wind, catch the glisten of winter sun, and enjoy.

Stuffed, Cuddly Friends

Often the hurt we feel comes from a place in us that is quite vulnerable, more childlike. We come into the world with wide-eyed innocence, and it is often rudely shattered. We learn to cope, but we never completely recover. Even as adults, we are often shocked at how mean the world is. Sometimes, we are the targets of such pain. No matter how together we seem, it can bruise us deeply and cause great doubt. At such moments, we need comfort and a way to safely talk over our hurt. If no one is available, a wonderful teddy or other stuffed animal can be a special friend. They do not doubt us or question our feelings. They are there when we need them, and they love being held. We can sleep with them, pack them in suitcases, and no one need know.

Join A Support Group

Being with others who are dealing with the same kind of stresses can make it easier to get through tough times. As our culture more readily acknowledges how difficult emotional challenges are for people to get through, a wider variety and greater abundance of support groups have sprung up everywhere. (And if there isn't one, we can start one.) It feels awkward at first, stepping into a room full of strangers. Others seem to talk so easily. Why would anyone want to listen to us? But once we take the plunge, share a bit of what we're feeling, and get the warm caring of strangers, we get a different perspective. It is amazing how a willingness to support and be supported can create a bond and sense of hopefulness in the face of impossible circumstances.

Someone To Listen

There are compassionate and professional people whose job it is to listen to us when we need a comforting and wiser perspective. They are available to us if we seek them out. A minister or rabbi, a counselor or therapist, or even a intuitive friend, can often be very helpful when we are all churned up. By talking things over, we can sort out what we are feeling and why, the options we have, and how we might make things different in our lives. When we are gripped by an emotion, we often see our situation quite narrowly. By getting things out in the open and considering other viewpoints and fresh solutions, we can often positively impact our situation. Instead of airing our dirty laundry when we talk about hurts as many of us were taught, we are healing deep wounds.

Scream It Out

The anger and rage we sometimes feel is unbelievable. Whether something infuriating occurred, or it built up over time, or we are holding old rage that gets triggered by current people or events, we need a sane and non-violent outlet. We get very little instruction about what to do with such intensely negative feelings. Usually, we see people stuff it or let it out in some cruel way. Neither is healthy. Try hopping in your car and driving, hopefully where the traffic is not too thick. Start talking about what is bothering you. (Night is perfect because no one can see.) When you feel the rage come up, scream as loud as you can. Repeat this until some of the intensity drains away. You may find yourself crying because underneath there is often deeper hurt.

Blowing Bubbles

When we are having a hard time figuring out what we feel or if we are depressed, a $.99 bottle of bubble soap from the dime store is often a perfect remedy. This strategy is great anywhere, anytime. (In fact, in cold climates, it's fun to watch bubbles freeze. You can pick them up—even giant ones.) Try sitting on your back stoop and gently blow bubbles. Notice how the rainbow colors sparkle. See how many you can blow at once, or how big a single bubble can get. A wire hanger bent in a circle, and dipped in a big pan of bubble stuff makes *huge* bubbles and bubble strands. You can twirl or run with the bubbles for additional delight. While bubbles might not fix our problems, they can bring us a smile in the middle of darker moments.

Healthy Competition

Healthy competition gets us revved up and challenges us to work at our peak ability. As people have gotten more interested in health and body fitness, the variety and availability of playable sports has sky-rocketed. There is something to fit everyone's personality, ability, schedule, and budget. From golf, baseball, basketball, volleyball, football, soccer, softball, polo, croquet, horseshoes, bocci ball, hockey, in-line skating, gymnastics, racquetball, skiing, and lap swimming to darts, and even archery, the possibilities are many. While we play, we breathe hard, we focus our minds, we work our bodies, and we have fun. Meanwhile, our creative minds can stew on the things that need fixing in our lives.

r.r.muggler
96

A Cheering Fan

Watching experts play the games we love can be vastly entertaining.
It can transport us away from the troubles at hand. In fact, women
often complain that this strategy is over-used by the men they care for!
Nevertheless, a good game offers a great escape and a source of great
pleasure. There is something inspiring watching an individual or a
team face a challenge, pull together, and win against the odds. We
celebrate these achievements with playoffs, championships, and the
International Olympics. Perhaps it reminds us that we, too, have
the ability to endure, break through obstacles, and surmount the
seemingly impossible.

Pictures Of Life

When you are roaming around the house not knowing what to do with your tension, pull out that box of pictures that has been accumulating for months and years and get ready to organize your photos. This is a project into which you can get immersed. While it may take you more than one evening, getting out photos that capture fun times with friends and family, special get-togethers, vacations, and other important events is a very healing activity. It reminds us of our connections. It puts the day-to-day grind in perspective. It opens our hearts and inspires us to find ways to honor the people who are important to us. Plus, it's fun. Putting page after page in an album that you can look at again and again is highly relaxing and heart-warming.

A Good Sweat

Hard, physical activity to the point of breaking a sweat, is a good way to deal with frustration. Clearing land, cleaning the house, lifting boxes, moving rock, and pushing around furniture are all good ways to get our bodies moving when we feel stuck. We breathe deeply and bring fresh air into our whole body. In turn, our bodies send out old toxins back out through sweat and heavy breathing. This makes us feel better. In fact, the therapeutic value of sweat is recognized widely in northern and Native cultures through the use of saunas and sweat lodges respectively. When you are feeling out-of-sorts inside, work until you sweat, take a sauna at a local health club, or look for someone in your area who offers a sweat lodge experience.

Purifying Energy

Have you noticed how people who are really upset have an unpleasant "vibe?" This is true for all of us. This may be due to our bodies chemically reacting under stress or to subtler shifts in energy that correspond to our moods. Many cultures believe that we benefit from purification when we get out of balance this way. Think how the Catholic tradition involves burning of frankincense and myrrh, traditions from India use sandlewood and other incense, and Native Americans smudge with sage and cedar, all to purify people and the environment. If you are feeling filled with uncomfortable energy, or if you have been surrounded lately by others who are, you may want to light some incense or buy a smudge stick to burn around your body and your home or office.

Busy Hands, Calm Heart

Handicrafts are as old as the hills. From basket weaving to looming cloth, from throwing pots and carving wood, from crocheting lace to building furniture, humans have been making things for their usefulness, beauty, and simple satisfaction. Gone are the days when we have to make our own soap, butter, or footstools. We can buy anything we need. But in doing so, we lose the crafts that were once handed down through generations. We also miss the artistic satisfaction which comes from creating. Yet many women still know the calming effect of picking up a needle to quilt, needlepoint, and knit. Many men still tinker with cars or keep a workbench in the garage or basement for projects. And now with gender roles changing, we can try anything!

123

Take Up A Hobby

We have a great deal of creative potential that never gets expressed. Not using our talents can leave us bored and under-challenged. This is one of the reasons why many people feel stress. They have not found work that allows them to express themselves fully, and so they feel frustration with their lives. Finding something that interests us enough to become a hobby, can give us a focus for our creativity and bring great satisfaction. When we've had a hard day, it is great to be able to change gears and do something completely different. New parts of our brain are stimulated, and we can get out of the rut of our routines. We get excited and intrigued, feeling more alive and vital. In short, hobbies have the wonderful effect of relaxing us.

A Loaf Of Bread

Did you know that your grandmother was working out her frustrations secretly while she was baking bread? Having a warm, gooey, sticky, and stiff knot of dough under our hands to push and pull is a wonderful way of working out things that bother us. . .and it gives us a delightful and delicious loaf of bread in the end. That dough needs us to work it hard, and we can definitely use an outlet for our aggressions. What a perfect match! This means, of course, that we have to bypass our electric breadmakers. While this wonderful machine is convenient for modern life, we completely miss out on the therapeutic quality of making our own bread from scratch.

Give Of Yourself

When we feel trapped by our lives and need a sense of renewal, there is nothing so revitalizing as volunteering for a cause we care about. Whether we donate our time and effort to a food shelf, shelter, nursing home, ecology group, arts organization, scout troupe, parkland, humane society, or neonatal intensive care unit, the act of giving is more than repaid with the emotional rewards we receive in return. Volunteering is inspiring. It teaches us. It shows us a side of life that we might not otherwise know. It gets us outside our own little sphere of trouble, however difficult it is to handle. We see that others have trouble, too, and usually, we are grateful for the hand we have been dealt. It could have been a lot worse, and we count our blessings.

Out Goes The Old Stuff

When we are ready to change, it is incredibly therapeutic to clean out drawers, closets, and storage areas to get rid of clutter and things we have outgrown. The urge to change hits us and makes us feel edgy, bored, ready for something different. If everything stays the same, it is hard to bring in the new. Somehow, symbolically, the act of getting rid of what we no longer need gets us ready for what is to come. It unburdens us of the old and lightens our load. So for those fidgety, "can't put your finger on what's bothering you but you sure need something to happen" moods, try an overhaul on your personal stuff. Besides, holding a tag sale and making a few bucks or doing a good deed by donating unused goods to a charity has its own satisfaction!

Solve A Puzzle

Having a puzzle started on a card table or the end of the kitchen table is an invitation to sit down for a few minutes and unwind. Trying to find pieces that fit gives us a welcome break from heavy demands of modern life and lets us calm down when we are steamed up. It lets our mind stew on troubles while we take a little break. Solving a puzzle has a challenge to it, so it is often satisfying for our creativity which may not have many other outlets. Good puzzles can be done over and over and still retain their challenge. They also offer an opportunity for members of the family to work together, converse, or simply sit in the same place peacefully. And an especially appealing puzzle can always be covered over with a layer of craft glue and framed.

A Good Cry

Society judges crying as one of the few acceptable outlets for women's stress; and it mistakenly ordains crying as off-limits for men. It is time for a different understanding. In truth, it is a wonderful way for *anyone*—male or female—to let out sadness and get ready to move on. A good cry is like a good storm. It bursts through when tension or distress is at a peak. When it's over, we have cleared the air. We feel different—perhaps drained, but certainly less overwhelmed by pain. It is important to not get trapped in the sadness forever: we seek release so that we can keep on growing. It might be tempting to feel sorry for ourselves and get stuck in self-pity. But this gets old for everyone. Besides, our lives are our own to shape. Nothing happens unless we keep going.

Hug A Tree

Some Native Americans hugged pine trees when they were upset. Whether we hug a tree or just lean up against one, the strength of a living giant can seep in and recharge our tired batteries. There is nothing quite so peaceful as a grove of trees. Its silence and settled aura can fill the soul. Whether you find a tree in a park, along a river-bank, in a forest, or even in your own yard, a tree can be a great comfort. We might read a book while sitting at its roots or take a nap under the shade. Sitting with our back to a tree, eyes closed, is a good way to think through what troubles us. We can lay under the crown of leaves, look up through the patterned branches, catch glimpses of sky, and watch the birds and squirrels play. There is nothing so calming.

r. r. ruggles
96

131

Watch The River Flow

Life is full of changes. Some of them we expect, and others we don't. Adapting to new schools, moves, jobs, marriages, births, divorces, deaths, break-ups, loss, and financial woes is stressful. Sometimes, we just need to know how to keep going even when life takes twists and turns, or when we hit up against obstacles. Watching a river flow, an ocean tide rise and fall, or a lapping lake is a great remedy for such a situation. Water has the ability to find a way through no matter how many obstacles it meets. It flows over, around, between, changing its pace and course whenever it must. We go through life this same way, confronting surprises and moving forward, hopefully, with as much fluidity as we can muster.

Pulling Weeds

When our inner weeds seem about to choke us, we are in great need of some sorting and thinning out. To help us work on these inner feelings, a robust session outdoors could be just what we need. This is a great time to pull weeds in the flower beds or vegetable gardens, use a weed-wacker or clipper around the edgings, trim over-zealous bushes and trees, and clear out underbrush. It even might be time to get out a paint can for touch-ups on beach chairs, fencing, house trim, etc. Did you ever think that you might be doing self-therapy when you were working outside? It's a perfect outlet for those negative, dark moods that overtake us and too often hurt both ourselves and others.

A Spiritual Sanctuary

Taking sanctuary in a holy place can provide great comfort when we are tired and distressed. The inner spaces of many churches and cathedrals are built to hold a mystical and inspiring silence. Whether we are a member or not, it can be very healing to sit in such a place. And in many communities, religious buildings are still open to the public. No one disturbs us as we ponder or meditate over our situations. In fact, the setting may elevate our thinking and help us make peace with circumstances or look at them in new light. All spiritual teachings are founded on universal principles that aim to guide, comfort, and raise us toward higher possibilities.

A Hammock's Sway

If you have two poles or two trees where you live, you can hang a simple hammock which will await you anytime you need a retreat. Climbing into a hammock brings back simpler memories of childhood for many of us. It evokes a sense of relaxation as soon as we lay down, lemonade and magazine at our side. Some are even big enough for two or for parent and child, creating a natural place to cuddle and connect. The hammock gently rocks as we move, soothing us and holding us in a world where, too often, there seems to be little time for such indulgence. Yet we all need holding, rocking, and cuddling. What a simple way to add this comfort back into our lives.

New Learning

When we are bored and dissatisfied with our lives, we need to add new excitement and fascination. All of us have untapped potential, creativity, and intelligence that is rarely developed in ordinary jobs and daily routines. This can leave us feeling empty, restless, and resentful. Even though it is safer to stay in familiar routines, taking a class might just add some needed intrigue and stimulation in our lives. We are learning creatures, but sadly, our love of learning is squashed early when we get the message that keeping in line is more important than exploring who we might be. Well, it's never too late. So if you suspect that you might be bored to your very core, then find something that interests you and get back to learning!

A Cultural Shift

All of us get stuck in our own viewpoints from time to time. When we come up against problems, we stay in our same old ruts of thinking, feeling, and reaction. Then we wonder why our lives never change. Getting outside of ourselves by seeing how others think or what they do differently can be very enlightening. As communications technology gets better, the world gets smaller, bringing the many and varied cultures of the world closer to us. Contrary to what we might believe, other people often cherish quite different values, priorities, and approaches to problems. Learning about another culture—be it Aborigine, Native American, Mayan, or Masai or another country's traditions—opens our awareness and the possibilities for our lives.

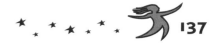

Write A Letter

People used to correspond much more than we do today. Our fast-paced life has made writing letters old-fashioned. Yet letters are a wonderful way to collect and express our thoughts and feelings with great care. If we are having a problem with someone—a boss, spouse, love, best friend, neighbor, politician, teacher, classmate, etc.—writing a letter might be a good outlet. First, freely express your feelings. Remember, you do not have to send the letter. You can keep it, burn it, mail it to yourself to read later after you've cooled down, or share it with a friend. You can even rewrite it as you gain new understanding. If you send it, it can be a quiet, simple way to express your feelings and let the other person respond with similar consideration.

A Pocket Pal

In earlier times, we might have worn or carried a protective amulet. Many still believe in good luck charms. Whether or not any beloved object can actually protect or bring luck, the comfort and inspirational power of a special momento is without dispute. Any meaningful object can keep us focused, give us courage, and alleviate stress. If it is portable, we can keep that comfort near us in a pocket, purse, briefcase, dashboard, office window, etc. A special stone can do the same thing. When you are particularly upset, go out for a walk to gain perspective. Along the way, look for an appealing rock to remind you of your new insight. When you find yourself wound up again, hold that stone to remember how you wish to change. It will ground and settle you.

A New Look

Usually when we are stressed, we could really use some nurturing. Our lives are out of balance in some way, and we probably aren't taking care of ourselves the best way possible. In such times, doing something to uplift and renew ourselves can be quite welcome. We need to get out of our rut and feel recharged. Sometimes, just a new haircut, manicure, outfit, tie, lipstick, or whole makeover will give us a bit of pick-me-up. Yes, it is superficial compared to the problems we face, but it affirms our right to be happy, silly, and to feel good even when we are struggling with bigger issues. This reminds us that we deserve to be treated well. It all starts with us: if we believe in treating ourselves well, we will attract others who treat us well, too.

Manicure, Pedicure

Many people find the relaxation and self-indulgence of a manicure completely refreshing. Male or female, this is a time to lean back and let another person massage, clean, and shape your fingernails or toenails. It is pure indulgence, pure frivolity, and pure relaxation. If this strategy fits into your schedule once a week or just once in a while, it is a simple and visible way to feel more handsome, beautiful, tailored, and together. Even a self-manicure can be a powerful way to let go of tension. The simple act of cleaning, shaping, and cutting our nails, gets us down to basics and away from bigger responsibilities for a short while. If we choose to adorn our nails with color, this can make it even more fun. Try new colors for extra delight.

A Nest Of Your Own

Just as taking care of our health makes us feel better, so does making sure that the environment in which we live expresses our unique personalities and meets our needs. Our room, apartment, or house is our cocoon. If it feels good, it will help us handle stress much better. Our home is where we go to unwind, rest, and recharge for the next day. Have you ever stopped to notice whether the space in which you spend your time feels good to you? What can you do to make it more nurturing? Does it need more color? A way to play music? More light? More plants? Take an especially close look at where you sleep. When you enter this room, does it feel cozy, warm, and inviting? This is your nest. Make it as comfortable and comforting as you can.

Spiff It Up

Giving our cars a good cleaning inside and out is positive therapy for anyone who is feeling overwhelmed by responsibility and stress. As we freshen up the vehicles that carry us, we are also putting ourselves back in order. It is hard to sort out our thinking if everything around us is chaotic. Often, we let our cars and trucks go because they seem the least of our priorities. Yet it only takes a day or two before the bottoms of our vehicles get littered with fast food garbage, gum wrappers, reminder notes, empty drink glasses, bottles, mail, magazines, papers from work, toys, etc., while the outside takes a beating from weather, roads, and construction. So, when you're wound up, get out the trash can, pail, vacuum, and car wax for a vigorous therapy session!

A Computer Break

When you feel like taking a swing at your boss, kids, spouse, or even the mailman, get your grumpies out with the latest version of *Duke Nuk'em 3D, Marathon, Doom,* or whatever is hot on your computer. Even a game of *Solitaire, Normality,* or *Hyper 3D Pinball* can get our minds off our troubles and calm us down. If you don't have access to computer games, go to a local emporium or theatre with video games. Or use a friend's *SEGA* or *Nintendo* to challenge yourself. Sparring on the screen instead of real life offers a constructive way to let out frustrations without hurting yourself or others. After you've calmed down, you can deal with the real problem with a clearer mind and less destructive energies.

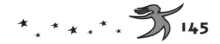

Build A Bonfire

Since humans discovered fire, they have been gathering around it to dance, sing, eat, worship, and commune with nature, God, and each other. When we've got the blues or are feeling confused, building a fire can be very healing. The simple act of gathering wood and making tinder from tiny sticks or newspaper helps us settle down. Building a structure of wood and tinder is satisfying, especially if it takes hold once we light it. The secret is using small pieces first and cross-layering the wood so there are plenty of air pockets. Whether we build fires in fireplaces, firepits, at campgrounds, in park fire-gratings, or along shores, the magnificent beauty and mysterious power of fire is incredible to watch—and it may inspire new solutions.

Laugh Away The Blues

Humor has a powerful ability to heal our bodies, minds, and hearts. When we laugh, our bodies produce "happier" chemicals, (endorphins), that actually can change not only our outlook, but our state of health. So when you find yourself down and out or overloaded with stress, get over to the local video store, search the comedy section, and take home some very powerful "medicine." With or without popcorn, laughing our heads off at silly screen antics is a lovely way to cause an emotional "paradigm" shift. We need release from the feelings that grip us, and this is much healthier than most of the more addictive ways we usually try. A funny book, cartoons, comic books, and stand-up comedy has the same effect. Go for it! You can't overdo this one!

Read Aloud

If we were lucky enough to hear stories read aloud when we were young, then we may remember how wonderful it is. Whether we are young or old, the wonder is the same. And being the reader is delightful, too. So find a story that you loved or that a librarian recommends, and try reading to a child. (You can always volunteer to read at a local library or school.) Grown-ups love this strategy, too. So with a friend, roommate, love, or spouse, pick a good story and give it a try. You can read a chapter at a time, in the car, before bed, or on a weekend picnic. It is even therapeutic to read to ourselves out loud, especially if it is something calming or inspirational. Or check out a book-on-tape at the local library for road trips or daily commutes.

A Simple Flame

Lighting a candle helps rekindle us when we feel overwhelmed or sad. We each have our own inner flame of hope which gives us the will to live. A candle flame symbolizes this inner hope and renews our spirit. Lighting a single candle while saying a simple prayer or affirmation touches our fundamental need to know that things will somehow be all right. They will. Things work themselves out eventually, and we will get wiser in the process. Meanwhile, we can light a candle every day to affirm our hope and prayers. Filling a room with candles and their soft light adds a gentleness at the end of the day or week that is a welcome change from demanding schedules. Life is not meant to be so gruelling, and this can affirm our willingness to find a way to change.

A Word Of Inspiration

Many others have walked these same roads before us. They faced trials and tribulations, they struggled to find their place in the universal scheme; they searched for their unique meaning and reason for being on the earth; and they got wiser in the process. Luckily, some of these people wrote down their thoughts during their journey. Their wisdom is collected in books of quotes and day-by-day handbooks. Beginning and ending our day with one or two quotes to which we can relate is deeply touching. They give us something to think about, something better to shoot for. They lift up our spirit, and help us keep to higher ground. These simple kernels of truth help us persevere when we might otherwise feel like giving up.

Monkey Games

The seriousness of life and our responsibilities has the power to over-whelm us and take away our joy and spontaneity. A good remedy for a burdened soul is a day at the zoo. Whether you go by yourself, with a friend, or better yet, a small child, you are in for a day of silliness and fun. Make sure you stop at the monkey habitat, because their antics will remind you of people you know. In fact, if you are having trouble with someone, find an animal that has similar qualities to both you and that person. What can you learn from them? What could you do differently? Animals have long inspired humans: look up the power different animals (bear, wolf, snake, buffalo, horse, turtle) represent for cultures such as Native American, Mayan, etc, to learn more.

The Rhythm Of Life

Every minute, our hearts beat 70 times, pumping blood through our bodies, keeping us alive. This pulse echoes in the rhythmical drum-work of all cultures. Modern life has taken us far from simple rituals involving drums and other traditional instruments, but people are re-discovering their power to revive and inspire. When you feel lethargic, stuck, lonely, or blue, pick up a drum. It can be a conga, tabla, or deerskin drum, an overturned pan or plastic pail, or even maracas or tambourine—anything to make noise. With a stick or spoon, find a rhythm you like: soft and slow, hard and deep, fast and intense. You may feel timid at first because it's so different than what you are used to. But drumming re-awakens ancestral rhythms deep in the soul.

Drop A Line

When we need to get away from it all and clear our minds, a simple pole with a bit of line and hook on it will often do the trick. Across America, people everywhere know about this age-old form of stress-management. It is peaceful. We get outside in the fresh air and sunlight and just sit. It is quiet. There is nothing to do except watch that line and, from time to time, cast it in again. Pure simplicity. It gets us away from the rush, noise, and push of our lives. We need that now and again. Plus, fishing gives us time to think. Time to reflect on our predicaments. It gives us space to unwind. A private place to grumble and cry without dumping on others. And if we actually catch something, we can look forward to mouth-watering morsels back at home!

Napping Away Fatigue

Just a few minutes with our eyes closed has the power to refresh us for the next part of our day. Fatigue is our enemy when we are under stress. It is harder to cope with any challenge when we are tired. The additional stress in turn creates more fatigue. This nasty cycle can undermine our ability to cope unless we get more rest. Besides making sure we get to bed early enough, adding cat-naps to our days is a big help. If we can lie down for fifteen minutes (use a timer if necessary), pull over to the side of the road and close our eyes a few minutes, or close the office door and zone out in our chair, we will feel more energy and alertness as a result. If you find yourself falling deeply asleep at such times, you need to get more sleep.

Serenade The Soul

Since the beginning of time, mothers have comforted their babies by humming or singing little made-up songs. Now that we're grown up, the right song at the right time can still change how we feel. So when we find ourselves in distress, we can give ourselves a little of that same comfort by singing. Humming a tune, singing in the shower, keeping time with the beat of a song, or singing along with the radio is very soothing. It is so easy and the impulse so natural. We don't have to be good or even able to carry a tune. But singing helps us express feelings that otherwise have a hard time coming out in regular conversation. Around the world, songs express both joy and pain. The next time you feel out-of-sorts, soothe yourself with a little tune.

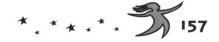

Bubble Away Troubles

When stress has gotten you all in knots, unwind with a fabulous jacuzzi experience. As you soak in warm water, powerful jets work over your tightened muscles and help them relax. The rushing, bubbling water carries your troubles away. When you come out, your body feels as if you had a massage. Jacuzzis have become so popular that most health clubs and even some hotels have them now. There are small portable machines to rent or buy which can be used with most tubs at home if you become a real fan of this technique. And of course, for those who can afford it, adding a hot tub with a jacuzzi for regular relaxation and pleasure is a healing aid to busy lifestyles.

A Personal Comfort Box

Any box, basket, drawer, or plastic keeper will work for this. Gather together a collection of things you can use for comfort: a good novel, a book of affirmations, candles, incense, aromatic oils, scented lotion, Chinese stress balls, favorite pictures, cookie fortunes, notes or letters from loved ones, pictures your kids made, special cards, bubble stuff, silly putty or clay, and comic books. Make sure it includes a copy of your 25 Personal StressBreakers™ list (which you make after reading *Dance Naked in Your Living Room*). Keep your comfort box handy for moments or days that are especially hard. Keep adding to it as you find new StressBreakers™. You can also make a comfort box for your kids or the whole family so that everyone has constructive outlets for stress.

Retreat To The Throne

If you live in a small space or with lots of people, you may find it difficult to get a few minutes to yourself. This is especially true if you have children or live with people who are physically or mentally challenged. There is little time for yourself. Others might interrupt or even resent you taking personal time to unwind. While we have to keep trying to get decent breaks, one almost certain place of escape is the bathroom. Even five or ten minutes behind a closed door can give us a welcome break. You don't actually have to be using the facilities: you can loosen your tie, take off your shoes, read a magazine, splash your face, or look out the window, do your nails, or plan what you are going to do next. A few minutes of peace is a precious thing.

Break Old Dishes

Aggressive anger can be very destructive if it is channeled the wrong way. But getting out feelings that fester and churn is important. A quiet strategy will not work for such feelings. In the movies, we see people punch walls or break chairs when they are enraged. This is too expensive for those of us who do not live on a movie set, so we have to find constructive substitutes. Buying old dishes at a thrift shop or tag sale and then smashing them in an empty garage or basement gives us great release when we are all steamed up. And it's easy to sweep up afterward. It doesn't hurt anything, anybody, or a leave lasting effect that we might regret. If we usually present a more polished and less emotional face to the world, no one has to know our secret strategy.

Fascinating Feathers

For a peaceful pastime that can take only a few minutes or a whole afternoon if you wish, take up bird-watching. This quiet sport is ever-more fascinating as we learn more about new species. We grow up recognizing the robin who heralds spring and maybe a blue jay, cardinal, gull, or sparrow. But there is a whole world of beautiful birds that live in the canopy above us, at the shore, or in wetlands, prairies, or deserts. Some of them are harder to spot or even quite rare. Having the chance to see such a bird is very exciting. Watching birds can even grow into a hobby, taking us to places we otherwise would never have visited. Taking time to look up in the trees and follow a birdcall, brings us down a notch or two from the normal rat-race of modern life.

r. r. ruggles
96

Doodle, Dots, & Crayons

Our children have a consummate ability to look on the bright side and keep rebounding from trouble. We were once like them. We still are inside, but it is buried very, very deep. When we need a little bit of sunshine and hope amidst our challenges, we can take lessons from little ones. Get yourself some crayons, markers, or colored pencils and get ready to return to childhood! Doodle, color in coloring books, connect the dots, or make your own pictures. It doesn't matter how good you are. In fact, using crayons is a good reminder that it is OK to go out of the lines! You will probably find yourself smiling at how silly and wonderful this feels. Watercolors and paint by number will do the same. What an inexpensive and enjoyable strategy!

Lost In A Daydream

While we are often chastised for wasting time in daydreams, day-dreaming is actually a very creative and healthy strategy for coping with stress. We don't have to be productive every single minute. Actually, our preoccupation with perfection and achievement is part of what gets us into trouble in the first place. When we take a few minutes to gaze out the window, dream at a desk, or sit on the couch doing nothing, we might just be recharging our batteries, stewing on new solutions, or taking a break from the day's intensity. This is immensely healthy for tense bodies and worried minds. And we can do it anywhere, anytime, and on any budget! Of course, doing nothing is also an over-used escape, so be careful not to get stuck in this one.

Chopping Wood

In the Far East, there is a legend of someone getting enlightened by the simple tasks of chopping wood and carrying water. We think of chopping wood as something for pioneers, woodsmen, and those who are naturally physical or who love the outdoors. But it works for anyone who needs to find another outlet for grief and anger. All it takes is an ax, a few blocks of wood, and some pent up energy. While we must always be careful to handle sharp blades safely, picking up an ax and pounding it down with all our might is very invigorating. And if we actually are splitting wood for a fire we might later use, it can be very satisfying. Chopping wood will get us breathing hard, work up a sweat, and leave us feeling strong enough to handle anything.

A Satisfying Squish

There is nothing so satisfying as the squish of marshmallows against the wall or windows when they are pitched at full speed. This is a strategy even a "nice" person can use without reproach. Nice people get mad, too, but have an even harder time expressing difficult or unpleasant feelings. Negativity is definitely not acceptable. But life evokes all kinds of feelings, many of them uncomfortable. So what's a nice person to do? Throw marshmallows, socks, feather pillows, stuffed animals, or even wadded up kleenex! No one gets hurt and no one has to know because this strategy can be virtually silent. If we want to yell and scream as we whip out each pitch, the strategy is even more potent. So get it out instead of covering it over. It'll feel better.

Look To The Stars

In the black of night, stars pierce through the darkness in an immense and unfathomable pattern. These same stars have been enchanting, inspiring, and guiding humans since the very beginning. When we feel lost, sad, completely frustrated, overwhelmed, lonely, or even bored, star-gazing can fill the void. All we have to do is step outside. A folding chair, blanket, or even plain earth gives us all the seating we need to watch and wonder. If we can get beyond city lights or to higher elevations, the intensity and beauty of the stars increases. This is a wonderful, private past-time. It helps us consider who we are and our place in the universe. It lets us commune with larger forces, take stock of what is important, and maybe make a wish on a falling star.

Comfy Old Clothes

Peeling off our clothes as we come into the door and immediately putting on our comfiest clothes helps transform our moods and our outlook. They can be the oldest, shabbiest, ugliest clothes that we wouldn't dare wear in public. Who cares? No one is going to see us. It's time to unwind, not impress. Climbing into clothes that create a cozy, nurturing feeling is a simple way to add some softness into our lives after a hard day. It takes us far away from the office, courtroom, roadways, competition, and commotion of all that we do. Add a good book, cup of tea, walk in the garden, or a few minutes on the front stoop, and we can settle way down.

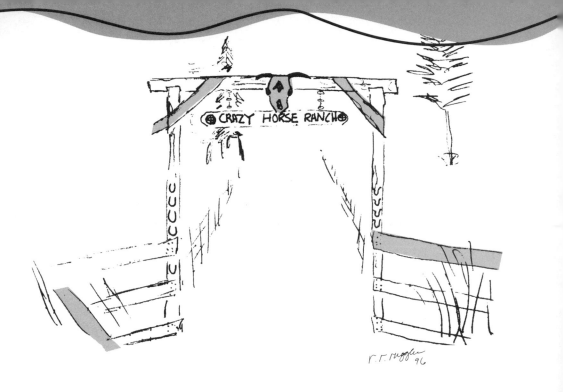

CRAZY HORSE RANCH

A Day In The Country

Sometimes we need a bigger get-away instead of just a quick remedy for stress. To counteract a crazy juggling of responsibilities—including job, family, romance, home, health, spirituality, and personal growth—we need to take a few steps back, switch gears, and get to a place without demands. Pack up and head away from the hub-bub of daily life. Out to the open spaces. Where a divine magnificence that defies words but moves us deeply still reverberates. Wide open plains with big sky. Towering mountains, silent and old. The ocean, full of mystery, amazingly powerful. Mystical forests, with immense quiet and dappled light. Rivers running free and wild. Out here, we sense our true selves. We remember our purpose. We find center once more.

Push Around Furniture

Have you ever known people that keep re-arranging their living spaces or offices? Maybe they are satisfying some artistic urge, but they may also be secretly letting off steam. Tussling with a heavy couch, rug, or shelf, is a great way to push and shove out those grumpy, edgy, uncomfortable feelings that churn inside without relief. When you really need to let off steam, pick a room and try changing the furniture. You may have to try several configurations—which is all the better for letting off pent-up steam—before you end up with one you like. You may, indeed, put everything back where it was in the first place, but meanwhile, you end up feeling better.

Tug Of War

A rowdy game of tug of war—whether it is with people or animals—is a fabulous stress management strategy. It is so quick: pick up a rope, towel, or plastic toy and let a puppy or dog have at it. Within moments, it will enthusiastically oblige complete with all the growls and lunges we need to feel downright gritty. In fact, it's even better if we growl and lunge, too! We can even use a favorite blanket or toy with a child for a toned-down version of the same game. This way, it is much sillier and puts weightier matters back into the right perspective. And when we're at a gathering, we can rally together a few willing hands for a good old-fashioned rope pull.

Defy Gravity

Sometimes it seems impossible to escape circumstances: they have a grip that won't loosen no matter what we try. We are stuck, and we don't like it. Things are supposed to work out if we try our best and do what is right. Yet we can still face tough times. To escape, some people find it invigorating to turn everything upside down—literally—and get out of the grip of gravity for a few minutes. Whether we practice yoga or gymnastics until we can do a headstand against a wall, or whether we hang upside down on a monkey bar or in anti-gravity boots, a few minutes looking at the world from an opposite point of view can be highly refreshing. Health experts even say that taking weight off our backs this way is good for our health. Whatever works!

A Good Punch

Feeling fit and capable of defending ourselves against any opponent is a powerful way to counteract the stress inherent in demeaning situations such as a stifling job, an abusive relationship, a lonely community, a belittling acquaintance, or an unsafe neighborhood. One way to feel more empowered against this is to take up boxing. We can buy a punching bag and gloves to use at home, or we can join a local gym where a coach can show us how to develop our physical power and improve our techniques so that we become stronger and more capable. Our growing sense of strength translates into better self-esteem and confidence which we carry into any environment. We do not have to put up with the unacceptable. Instead, we have the power of choice.

Go For A Ride

Getting away from it all for a little while after a heavy day can do us a world of good. How we travel isn't important: car, bike, motorcycle, sailboat, canoe, motorboat, moped, or even horse. They are all fun, go at a different pace, and take us to new scenery. Some take us at a quiet clip, slowing us down. Others make us feel like kids. Some give us a sense of power and release. A word of warning: too many of us are working out stress on roadways with aggressive, careless behavior. Just as we can hurt those we love with inappropriate negativity, we can hurt other people with careless driving. So please, take care. Everyone will appreciate it. If you are so depressed you don't care if you endanger others, get professional help before someone gets needlessly hurt.

Feel The Wind

In Chinese medicine, the power of the wind is well known. Most of us take it for granted. We enjoy a soft breeze on a summer's day, and we appreciate its ability to keep bugs away. Otherwise, we don't take much note. But standing in the wind, letting it blow over, around, and through us, can be very cleansing if we are chock-full of stress. Wind is elemental, just like water. It flows wherever it wants to go, finding its way around obstacles. It can be quite gentle or amazingly power-ful. Feeling a soft wind on our face can soothe away stress. Standing in the primal power of a hefty wind and letting our bodies wrestle with its force offers us a very effective way to get rid of pent-up stress. Add a yell, scream, or wail, and it's a great stress release.

Part 3:

Your Personal StressBreakers™ List

Personal StressBreakers™

Now, it's your turn. Using the suggestions in *Dance Naked In Your Living Room* or those you discover yourself, make a list of 25 healthy choices you can make when you are stressed. They have to fit you and all of your feelings and moods. Keep this list handy and use it as soon as you feel the agitation that makes you eat, drink, smoke, shop, gamble, work, pull away, get aggressive, get high, get laid—or even get too dogmatic. After you've cooled down, take time to find out what's bothering you and how you might make things better. Remember, this inner examination is best done in private or with a very trusted confidant. It takes a commitment to make such time in busy lives. The answers are often not easy to find, and what we discover may not be easy to look at. But if we don't do this, the agitation will surely return.

Your Personal 25 StressBreakers™

1.

2.

3.

4.

5.

6.

7.

8.

9.

10.

11.

12.

13.

14.

15.

16.   17.   18.

19.   20.   21.

22.   23.   24.

25.

Note: *If you copy this list onto a small notecard to keep in your wallet, on your bathroom mirror, refrigerator, or visor of your car it will be nearby when you need it. Good luck! And remember to make time to listen to what is upsetting you in the first place once you've settled back down.*

183

Dance Naked Books & Seminars

Living To Grow Talks

Presentations For Greater Insight, Joy, Self-Esteem, Trust, Confidence, & Compassion

By Rebecca Ruggles Radcliffe

People today feel the pressure of fast-paced lives which leave them vulnerable to stress, low self-esteem, and unhealthy choices. All of us need inspiration to discover healthier ways of living. Rebecca's presentations and work-shops provide inspiration and encourageme to creatively pursue personal growth and th process of finding joy. This exciting inner journey is both highly individual and amazingly universal.

Sample Keynotes/Topics
◆ About to Burst™: Ending Violence, Finding Ho
◆ Dance Naked In Your Living Room: Handling Stress and Finding Joy
◆ Lives in Balance: Choices Toward Wellness
◆ Living To Grow: Choosing To Be Conscious, Courageous, and Creative
◆ Our Inner Spirit: Nourishing Our Souls
◆ Learning To Live In Our Bodies: Changing Emotional Eating and Body-Hatred

For: Women's events, Keynotes, Wellness Fairs, Workshops, Panel Discussions, Talks, Presentations, In-Services, Professional Training, Luncheon Lectures, Women's History Month, "Celebrating Every Body" Week, Addiction/Violence Prevention, Orientation, Men's Groups, PTOs, Corporate Conferences, Commencements, Assemblies

About Rebecca Ruggles Radcliffe

Rebecca Ruggles Radcliffe is a national lecturer and workshop leader on stress, personal growth, self-esteem, joy, body-image, and emotional eating. She is Executive Director of EASE™ Publications and Resources, an organization dedicated to enhancing personal growth and self-esteem. Rebecca has spoken at many community health events, colleges, universities, national conferences, corporations, retreats, and seminars.

Call for Information

If you are interested in receiving a brochure on Rebecca's speaking or to discuss having her conduct a program for your organization or community, call at (800) 470-GROW (4769) or (612) 825-7681.

185

Dance Naked In Your Living Room: Handling Stress & Finding Joy

By Rebecca Ruggles Radcliffe

Dance Naked In Your Living Room is a playful, positive tool for inspiring personal growth and decreasing the destructive impact of stress on people's lives. *Dance Naked*™ helps us discover healthy ways to deal with the challenges of life—and change old patterns of overeating, drinking, overworking, compulsive shopping, aggression, drug use, or depression. By learning how to nurture ourselves better and listen to our needs and dreams, *Dance Naked*™ puts us on a journey of greater joy. A great additon to your personal wellness collection or gift for friends, co-workers, & family.

"A delightfully simple approach to the high-pressure stress that plagues us all!"

**About To Burst™:
Handling Stress & Ending
Violence—A Message for Youth**

by Rebecca Ruggles Radcliffe

Young people today face more stress than any other generation. They turn to drinking, drugs, sex, violence, eating disorders, depression, and other destructive choices to cope. *About To Burst*™ is a hip, creative book that helps youth learn to positively deal with stress—without harming themselves or others. By showing young people creative alternatives to use when life gets tough, this book offers a radically simple solution to help prevent violence and self-destructive choices. A great tool for parents, educators, counselors, and anyone who cares about young lives.

*"What a big help for the pressure young people feel
in a world filled with stress, addictions, violence,
and broken dreams."*

EASE17

**Enlightened Eating™:
Understanding and Changing
Your Relationship With Food**

By Rebecca Ruggles Radcliffe

Enlightened Eating™ is an insightful and supportive book on overeating, weight, and body-image for those who struggle with eating issues and feel self-conscious about their bodies. *Enlightened Eating™* compassionately explores how stress, eating, body-image, and self-esteem are so closely linked while inspiring and encouraging healthier life choices. Complete with 34 exercises for making personal change, *Enlightened Eating™* is used by individuals, support groups, and counselors nationwide.

" This is the best book I've read on the subject!"
"It has made a huge difference in my life."

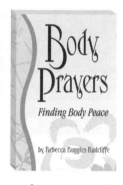

Body Prayers: Finding Body Peace—A Journey of Self-Acceptance

By Rebecca Ruggles Radcliffe

Body Prayers™ takes the reader through an inner journey about society's obsession with thinness and the harmful effect it has on self-esteem. Through this exploration, females of all ages are helped to question our narrow definition of beauty and find greater self acceptance for their bodies. Ending on a poetic and inspirational note, *Body Prayers*™ affirms every woman's right to embrace her unique beauty and to express her talents in the world which so desperately needs feminine perspectives today.

*"Soulful, heart-warming, and uplifting.
This is a breath of fresh air!"*

The Enlightened Eating™ Tape Set

Four heart-warming, uplifting introductory discussions to trigger new insights and understanding on emotional eating, body hatred, eating disorders, & inner meaning.

" Such a private and easy introduction!"

Developing Healthier Eating Habits

A practical pocket-guide to creating new eating patterns to help those with eating issues begin to make positive change. Excellent handout.

"A great help for students & clients"

Anorexia & Bulimia: The Silent Struggle

An intimate and personal video discussion on eating disorders, how they affect the body, their causes, treatment, and what friends or family can do to help. For small group or individual viewing. 29 min. A quiet version of Rebecca's popular talk. No rentals or previews.

" A compassionate introduction to eating disorders and the struggle to recover."

**Order by phone: 1-800-470-4769 fax: 1-612-226-5641 e-mail: brdrrr@bitstream.net
Mail: EASE, P.O. Box 8032, Mpls. MN 55408. Purchase orders accepted. No credit cards.**

✿ EASE™ Resources

- ❑ *Body Prayers™*, $15.00
- ❑ *About to Burst™*, $15.00
- ❑ *Enlightened Eating™*, $18.95
- ❑ *Dance Naked In Your Living Room™*, $12.00
- ❑ *Enlightened Eating™ Tape Series*, $19.95
- ❑ *Anorexia & Bulimia: The Silent Struggle™*, $39.95
- ❑ ____ copies of *Developing Healthier Eating Habits* (see chart below)

Quantity	Price	Quantity	Price
1	2.50	21-35	1.00 ea.
2-9	2.00 ea.	35+	.75 ea.
10-20	1.50 ea.		

✿ Shipping & Handling

For order totals of:	Add:	For order totals of:	Add:
$3.00 to $20.00	$4.00	$81.00 to $100.00	$8.00
$21.00 to $40.00	$5.00	$101.00 to $120.00	$9.00
$41.00 to $60.00	$6.00	$121.00 to $140.00	$10.00
$61.00 to $80.00	$7.00	$141.00 or more... add 8% of your order total	

- ❑ I have enclosed a check for $_____ made payable to EASE™ (U.S. dollars only)

- ❑ Send check and order form to:
  EASE™, P.O. Box 8032, Mpls, MN 55408-0032. Allow 3-6 weeks for delivery. Thank you! Questions? 1-800-470-4769

- ❑ **Please add me to your private mailing list.**

PLEASE PRINT CLEARLY:

Name (Individual name required for tracking orders)

Address (Please use street address for UPS orders)

Title

City   State   Zip

Organization

Phone Number (Include for questions about your order)

"Just do what you want.
If people laugh at you,
just go on playing."

Chloe, at age 4½